Leo and Gregory: Shapers of the Church

By Catherine Gunsalus González

Contents

Introduction

Many Protestants believe the church could well do without popes. Therefore, why study two of them? Leo the Great and Gregory the Great: Would *we* call them *great*? Or is that a term only Roman Catholics would use?

This brief study will introduce two leaders of the church who were instrumental in bringing both power and prestige to the office of the bishop of Rome. Our study is not of the papacy, however. It is a study of two leaders who would have been great assets to any church and who have much to teach us about faithfulness and leadership in difficult circumstances.

This book is also a story about ourselves. No matter how far apart Protestants and Roman Catholics have been for the last four centuries, we were one church for fifteen hundred years. And that earlier history has influenced all of us.

Protestants did not rid themselves of the entire past when they formed new churches. Though they were reacting strongly to problems in the church of the fifteenth and sixteenth centuries, what happened in the centuries before that time still deeply affected them. The early Protestants were inheritors of patterns and understandings of the church and the world that had been part of church life for more than a thousand years.

To that common ancient heritage we turn in this study. That heritage is our history, not someone else's. Knowing that history helps us know who we are and who we have been. And knowing that history gives us some clarity in thinking through who we, as the church, should be in the future.

1

Two Giants in Rome

In this book we will deal with two people who, though distant in time from twentieth-century Christians and even more distant in policies from Protestants, have nonetheless had a major influence on the whole church. They were gifted individuals who used all their abilities for the sake of the church they were called to lead. From them we can gain some significant insights into what being Christians in a rapidly changing society means.

Leo I and Gregory I were both bishops of Rome. Both have historically been referred to as "the Great" and for good reason. About a century and a half separated their work. Leo was born about 390 and died in 461. Gregory's birth occurred about the year 540, and his death was in 604. Enormous changes took place in the surrounding culture during that relatively brief period. Yet, in many ways an author could write a single biography and, with a simple changing of the names, have it do in outline for both popes.

Before we look at what Leo and Gregory had in common, however, a glance at the differences will set the stage for the changes that occurred in the life of the Western church between 450 and 600.

The Significant Differences

Much happened in the years between Leo's death and Gregory's time as pope. The situation in the

4

Western part of the Roman Empire deteriorated considerably. New groups of invaders pushed through the borders and devastated much of Italy.

Though both Leo and Gregory understood themselves to be part of the one Roman Empire, Leo lived his life in terms of that relationship. His world was still the Mediterranean world of that empire, though with some invasions from outside.

Gregory lived in a different world, a world that included barbarian groups pressing from the North and the West. Gregory's world was increasingly centered in the North and West rather than focused toward the East and the emperor. Gregory had grown up in the turmoil of war and siege, of famine and plague; these were also constant elements of his time as pope. War and famine were no longer novel events that could be considered to be interruptions in an otherwise peaceful continuation of the Roman domination of the Mediterranean world. The barbarians were clearly a permanent and massive part of any future that existed.

In the midst of the turmoil, a strong interest in monastic life had developed, culminating in Benedict's formulation of his *Rule* for monastic communities. Monasteries were havens of sanity and sometimes safety in the midst of a world that was increasingly subject to destruction. The fragility of life and the insecurity of riches made such monastic life attractive.

As a relatively young man, Gregory gave up his wealth and position in order to become a monk. He was the first monk ever to become pope. For him, having to leave the monastery in order to take a position of power in the church was a great trial rather than a privilege. He loved and understood monastic life. Leo had had no such inclinations. Monasticism was not strong in Italy during his lifetime. This fact was a major difference in the lives of the two men.

Another distinction between these two people can be traced to the role of the barbarians in Gregory's perception of the future. Gregory realized the barbarians were a permanent part of the Empire and felt an urgent need to evangelize these Germanic groups. Some of these people were already Christians but belonged to a form of Christianity that the people of the Empire considered heretical.

In many cases, whole tribes had been converted when their king or leader decided to become a Christian. However, the people themselves did not freely decide to become Christians. As a result, their faith was often quite shallow. Gregory spent much of his energy working with these people. He also devoted much effort to attempting to win to the faith those persons who had never been part of the church and to winning the Arians to the Roman Catholic faith. These Arians were followers of Arius, a leader whose views on the Trinity the Council of Nicaea had condemned in 325. Gregory had the heart of a missionary. His work in this field became pivotal for the future of Europe, as we shall see later in our study.

When we put together Gregory's concern for missions and his involvement in monasticism, we find a powerful combination. Gregory saw the potential for missionary work done by monks. He developed this vision and gave monasticism a new task. Rather than seeking to escape from a world in turmoil, monks were to be the instrument of the church for the conquering of that turmoil and for uniting the Romans and the barbarians in one church. Leo, though not opposed to missions to the barbarians, never felt this concern as deeply as did Gregory. Leo's times and the demands were different.

Leo's problems included critical issues of doctrine that were dividing the church. The controversies and the divisions were mostly in the Eastern, Greek-speaking area of the Empire; but Leo was vitally involved as one who could act as an arbiter and as a bearer of the ancient tradition of the Western branch of the church. Leo was a theologian, one of the most astute of his time. He was of critical importance in the final rendering of the church's understanding of the relationship of the divinity and the humanity of Jesus. To this subject we shall also return later.

Gregory was a significant theologian for the church after his time, but his work was quite different from Leo's. Gregory was not what can be called a creative theologian. He really had few doctrinal issues to debate. The need during Gregory's time was for a clear, simple statement of Christian beliefs, for a strong pastoral sense regarding how the church's teachings make a difference in the lives of people, and for helpful words on how to plant the church in new areas. Gregory wrote not for theologians but for new Christians and for those who had little theological background. His work was practical, not original. But it was and is very useful to the church.

The Similarities

Both Gregory and Leo can truly be called popes. We do not need to rehearse the long and confused history by which the bishop of Rome became known as the pope, but both Leo and Gregory understood and defended their role as patriarch of the Western church. They also assumed a certain pre-eminence over patriarchs in the Eastern church, although Christians in the East did not fully recognize or acknowledge their pre-eminence. We shall return to this matter later in our study. But both Leo and Gregory were popes in the sense that we generally understand the term today. They were popes far more clearly than their predecessors had been.

Both Leo and Gregory were in office during periods of constant invasion of Italy by Germanic and Asiatic tribes. Both men were responsible for dealing with the leaders of these groups. Both negotiated terms of

7

withdrawal of barbarian forces from Rome in the absence of any really viable civil authority. Both Leo and Gregory were thrust into the role of political leadership due to a vacuum of political power. The Roman Empire was crumbling in the West. No one else had the power or prestige to deal with the invaders. Doing so often meant using the church's funds to pay for the terms of withdrawal. None of the popes before or between Leo and Gregory—and few after them—had the power and ability to carry out such political tasks.

Both Leo and Gregory were Roman. Not only had both been born in or near Rome, both had absorbed to the very marrow of their bones the essential character of Roman culture at its best.

All societies have some structure of law, customs, and rules by which the community lives in reasonable harmony. To some degree the strong must be limited in their power over the weak, and the weak must receive certain rights. Roles of various groups of people within the society and their relationships need to be clarified. Rights in regard to property must also be set forth. This need applies to all human societies, whether it is met by written codes or by customs that have the force of law.

Roman culture had carried the clarification and elaboration of such laws and the structures for their enforcement to great heights. Clear definitions, written codes, and precedents of interpretation were of major concern. The roles of magistrate and judge were of great importance. In fact, the legal definitions of rights, responsibilities, and relationships were central to the society.

These definitions had also become central to the interpretation of Christianity that had developed in Latin culture. Latin, a language of great precision, had been the vehicle for the development of Roman law. Even in the Greek-speaking areas of the Roman Empire, Latin was the language of the courts and of the judicial process.

People well trained in this aspect of Roman culture

excelled in the ability to clarify arguments regarding relationships, issues of authority, and the demands of justice within these contexts. These people understood the structures and procedures of good administration. Both Leo and Gregory possessed these characteristics beyond the range of most of their contemporaries. Thus when in the papal office, Leo and Gregory carried enormous authority in areas of civil government as well as in the sphere of church administration.

Both popes were quite concerned to maintain and clarify the power of the papacy and to define the role of the pope in relation to other bishops. Both were accustomed to a hierarchical structure of society, so they expected a hierarchy to operate within the church as well. The development of papal power was an unsurprising aspect of this hierarchical form of administration.

Both men were also Roman in that they felt themselves to be part of the Roman Empire, which in their time was centered in Constantinople. They recognized the authority of the emperor and were in contact with the imperial court. The Empire was a single reality, though the West was declining as the center of power as the culture of the Eastern part of the Empire, the Greek part, gained in status.

These two popes were concerned with the purity of the church, both in terms of the morality of its members and the orthodoxy of its teachings. Leo and Gregory used their administrative ability and their understanding of the power of the office that they held to further the ends of the purity of the church in these respects. This fact does not mean that they sought to undermine other offices. The Roman legal structure that they both represented led them to support lesser officers, such as other bishops, abbots, and civil officials , and to call them to carry out the tasks of their offices. Gregory and Leo were both reformers who used the structure of the church as they understood it to maintain or restore the holiness and truth that the church should possess.

9

The Significance for Us

The church does not invent totally new forms of government for itself. No matter how often churches attempt to prove that their forms of government are what Jesus or the apostles intended, the course of history shows that churches develop their forms of government on the basis of options the surrounding society presents to them.

However, the church does not take over such forms uncritically. The church adopts various secular models and uses them to work out its mission and purposes. The gospel supplies norms for this adaptation process. Thus, a church in the midst of the Roman Empire would turn to the Roman model in developing its own internal structure. In the work of Leo and Gregory, we see two bishops of Rome who understood that structure is necessary in order for the church to exist and to be the church.

We belong to an age that is quite different in terms of the options available in political and in governmental life. Many people do not care for monarchical forms—rule *by one person*—whether in state or in church. But this attitude is a modern development. Rule by one person was the major form of political style in the ancient and in the medieval world, whether that one person was born to office (as in the case of kings), took office by military force (as in the rule of a general), or was appointed to office by some very limited group of officials. Monarchy was the typical form of civil government during the first six centuries of the church's existence. We tend to forget that fact.

For Protestants, the break with the Church of Rome occurred at the time of the development of alternative forms of government. Republicanism and its representative forms was in the air in the sixteenth century, especially in areas of Europe where trade and commerce were growing rapidly. Nationalism was also breaking up the earlier imperial structures in Europe. Therefore, the majority of Protestant churches whose roots go back to the sixteenth century demonstrate both republicanism and nationalism.

Most Protestant churches are nationally organized in the sense that their highest legislative body is coterminous with national boundaries and the forms of government include elected representatives to major legislative bodies. However, these factors are qualified by two modifications that make church structure different from the secular model.

First, a recognition that the "one, holy, catholic church" includes those churches outside national borders is always present. Therefore, some expression of connection between the national church and other churches must be made (though this connection is often more symbolic than effective and real). Second, because the church must maintain the purity of its message, the clergy usually have a clear role in the determination of who is to be ordained for the office of preaching.

At the present time, the Roman Catholic Church and several others still follow forms of monarchical government. Some Protestant churches follow republican forms. But both forms are altered to meet the specific needs of the Christian community.

We live in an age that is no longer fully committed to either form. Increasing nationalism, as well as increasing global awareness, add to the confusion, since such factors pull the churches in contradictory directions. Both Roman Catholic and Protestant churches have yet to deal with the issues that these changes in the surrounding culture raise for the internal life of the church.

What we can learn from both Leo and Gregory is that the church is related to the society in which it develops in terms of the forms of government it chooses and that forms of government can be the means of reform within the life of the church. Reform does not have to come from outside the structures. It can be the result of the faithful use of decent, secular structures of government. Wise administration and a clear understanding of the workings of government

11

and the purposes and powers of various offices can bring about a significant renewal and revival of the church.

Neither Leo nor Gregory really revised the form of the church. Both, however, used the structures that existed with clarity, with purpose, and with consistency in order that the church might more nearly fulfill its purpose.

These popes retained the clearly Roman view of the purposes and power of good administration at a time when the Empire had lost it. In the West in particular, corruption and greed had undermined the social fabric, aiding and abetting the collapse of the society and the success of the invaders. These popes and the structures they developed became the inheritors of this ancient tradition and transmitted it to those peoples who had never been a part of old Roman culture.

Some Issues for Today

Before we begin our study of these two giants in the church, can we set the stage by reflecting on the kinds of issues their ministry raises for us?

First, can we see ways in which our own church shows the marks of the culture in which it grew and developed? Should the church use secular models for its own life? Can we see parallels between our situation and the situation of the church that Leo and Gregory led? Must the church keep changing, or should it stay with the form it took at its beginning? What are the problems we see at the moment in our own church life because of different views about how decisions ought to be reached in the church?

Second, why does the church have organization and structure? How can we judge if the church is working well or not? How does reform come about in the church? Do some structures make reform easier? Do some structures make reform harder? Why?

Third, how do new challenges change the shape of the church? Think of missions to the barbarians and the development of a missionary monasticism during Gregory's time. What challenges in our own era does the church need to face? What new structures or new ways of organizing our life together could we use to meet these challenges?

2

Leo as Church Leader

We know little about Leo's life before he became a major church official. His birth date was probably in the last decade of the fourth century, perhaps as early as A.D. 390. We do not know much about his family either. One tradition suggests that the family lived in Tuscany (a region in northwest Italy), and clearly Leo had as solid a literary education as was possible at the time.

The Western half of the Roman Empire had been weakened through repeated invasions by various barbarian groups. The emperor and the central government, located at that time in the Eastern portion of the Empire, could do little to defend the West. In 409, while Leo was a young man, the Empire ceased to be responsible for the defense of Britain since troops were needed elsewhere. In 410, the Goths captured and sacked Rome. When Leo was an adult, Roman North Africa, important for the production of food for Italy, fell victim to the Vandals. North Africa's major city, Carthage, fell in 439. Gaul and Spain also endured invasions by Goths and Vandals.

During this period of time, Leo was actively involved in the life of the church in Rome. In a letter, Augustine (the great North African theologian) referred to a Leo. At that time this person was an acolyte (one who assists a priest in the celebration of Mass) from Rome. In 418, this man was sent to North Africa to gather information for the bishop of Rome about the heresy called Pelagianism which was active in North Africa. We do not know if this person was the man who became known as Leo the Great, but he may very well have been.

By the decade of the 430's, Leo was known as one of the most able officials in the Roman church. Bishops and civil officials called on him, often seeking his aid in presenting issues to the pope. Leo had great credibility within Rome and far beyond.

In the year 440, Leo went to Gaul to try to negotiate between two quarreling Roman generals and to bring peace so that the defense of the Empire could continue. What an unusual role for a church official! The people and the civil government apparently had a great deal of confidence in and respect for Leo.

Not surprisingly, when the pope died while Leo was in Gaul, Leo was elected pope. Leo was the obvious choice. He left Gaul and returned to Rome where he was ordained a priest as well as a bishop on September 29, 440. Leo had been a deacon and an archdeacon prior to that time.

The Leader of the West

Once Leo became pope, his involvement in civil affairs grew. All Italy was terrified by the advancing Huns, a new group of invaders of Asian rather than European origin. Their leader, Attila, had already conquered other lands, and fearful tales had reached Rome. As Attila approached, Leo and two civil officials went out to meet him. They negotiated the release of hostages already taken and dissuaded Attila from taking the city. Attila then withdrew.

Whether Attila had other reasons for withdrawing

we do not know. But Leo certainly gained stature as a result of this event. Attila died the next year, and his kingdom collapsed. This occurrence added to the impression that Leo had God on his side.

Three years later the Vandals marched on Rome, and Leo went out of the city to meet with the Vandal king. Leo gained some concessions again, this time in terms of the lives and safety of the city's inhabitants. But he was unable to prevent the sacking and looting of Rome.

Both the role of Leo as the chief negotiator with the invaders and the recognition of his role by the barbarian leaders are astonishing. No one else in the West had the stature to negotiate in this way, and both the Romans and their enemies understood that fact.

The Huns were not Christians, though they had some knowledge of the church and probably some Christians were in their midst (perhaps the result of earlier raids into Roman territories and the taking of Christian slaves). The Huns bore no hostility toward the church in particular; and in fact, they seemed to sense that the leader of the church was a legitimate spokesperson for the society he represented. Leo took on this role as civil negotiator as a duty that he must perform. Leo's contemporaries saw him as the real leader of the West, and his authority extended far beyond the walls of the church.

None of these activities conflicted with Leo's sense of being a loyal subject of the Roman emperor (though at this point in history the emperor was a rather weak and ineffectual person). This emperor had indeed asked Leo to participate in the negotiations with the Vandal ruler. A distant and rather powerless emperor, even he recognized that Leo could do more than a civil official. The Empire might not have much stature in the eyes of the barbarians, but the church did.

The Leader of the Church

Within the life of the Western church, Leo's leadership was apparent from the moment he took office. But he faced many challenges. From Leo's letters we can catch a glimpse of the chaos resulting from invasions and disruptions. Leo's task was to bring order out of this chaos.

Italy had been invaded. Captives had been taken. Many Roman citizens were held for years before they were released. Some of these captives never returned. Family life was disrupted when people were taken away—and also when they were allowed to return. Often new marriages had been contracted by those left at home on the assumption that the one taken away was dead or would never return.

Leo's fairly rigid morality was quite obvious. We see this attitude in his decision about nuns whom the invaders had raped. Leo said that such nuns could no longer be enrolled as consecrated virgins of the church, though they were still to be part of a religious order. Leo also ruled that men who had married widows and who now were clergy had to separate from their wives, for priests could only marry virgins. (The demand that Roman Catholic clergypersons be unmarried did not come until later in the history of the church.) Priests who actually served at the altar could remain married as long as they lived with their wife as brother and sister, that is, without intimacy.

In areas other than sexual morality, Leo could also be quite rigid. He totally opposed the taking of usury, taking interest on a loan, by any Christians and most specifically by any clergy; nor were clergy to turn their business affairs over to others to manage by lending at interest so that they, the clergy, could reap the benefits.

Leo opposed Christians attending the games and spectacles that still occurred in Rome. Just after the Vandals had withdrawn from Rome, plundering the city but not attacking the inhabitants, Leo preached a sermon during a church service held to commemorate the return of the populace and their freedom from the Vandals. Leo was upset that very few people attended the service because they had gone to the circus games instead. He said,

17

Who was it that restored this city to safety? that rescued it from captivity? the games of the circus-goers or the care of the saints? . . . Return to the LORD, remembering the marvels which He has deigned to perform among us; and ascribing our release not, as the ungodly suppose, to the influences of the stars, but to the unspeakable mercy of Almighty GOD, Who has deigned to soften the hearts of raging barbarians.[1]

Leo was dealing with a populace that was only nominally Christian. Many people still continued in their earlier styles of life.

Leo wished to systematize processes throughout the church. He wrote to bishops indicating how elections within the church were to be held, who was elegible for specific offices, when ordinations could be held, when baptisms could be performed, and so forth.

In all his activities, Leo's desire was to have a church that was well run and consistent in its decisions. He wanted *one* church, uniform in its ways of doing things. Leo understood that as pope he was responsible for clarifying such procedures and for insuring such uniformity.

Leo did not create policy completely on his own. He drew on Roman church tradition and seemed generally to be imposing on areas outside Rome what had been Roman ways and forms. When Leo dealt with emergency situations or the results of the chaos in the Empire, he seemed to draw on the underlying rationale for procedures in the Roman church or created new policies in line with the theological foundations of the church.

From earliest times and through the fifth century as well, one of the tasks of a bishop was preaching. In fact, frequent preaching was a major way in which a bishop could educate and persuade the people. Before radio, television, and newspapers, people eagerly listened to the public statements by those in authority in order to learn what was happening in the world.

Sermons by leading bishops often had this character. Leo was an excellent preacher. His sermons were crisp, clear, easy to understand, direct, and related to the lives of his hearers.

Fasting was important to Leo. He urged the people to keep the fasts; but fasts were to be times for positive actions, not simply times to limit the intake of food. Giving to the poor, trying to improve relationships with others, and lessening the power of sin in the lives of Christians were all to accompany fasting.

In his preaching Leo constantly referred to the significance of baptism, to the whole of the Christian life, and to the meaning of community. Through all his preaching Leo sought to help people make their Christian life consistent so that they actually carried out in their life outside the church building what they professed in worship.

During Leo's time, probably in large measure due to his interest in liturgy and uniformity in church life, the worship of the Western church took on a more specifically Latin, Roman flavor. The original language of worship in the Empire was Greek, in the West as well as in the East. Most of the church's leaders spoke Greek, even in the West. In fact, many of the bishops of Rome had grown up speaking Greek. But the populace spoke Latin. By the beginning of the third century, the liturgy of the church was gradually being put into Latin; but the style of worship still had many Greek characteristics. With Leo, a liturgy developed that was characteristically Latin.

One major contribution of Leo to this process of making worship Latin was the creation of the form of prayer called a *collect*. This type of prayer is typically Latin in structure and deals with a single issue. If a collect occurred at the beginning of the service, it helped focus the worship on the specific issues or concerns of that day. We still use the term *the collect of the day*. One of the most familiar collects, dating perhaps to the eleventh century, has found its way into the worship of many churches: "Almighty God, unto whom all hearts are open, all desires known, and from whom no secrets are hid: Cleanse the thoughts of our hearts by the inspiration of thy Holy Spirit, that we may perfectly love thee, and worthily magnify thy holy name; through Christ our Lord. Amen."[2] Collects were usually one sentence in length, balanced in structure, and quite stylized in form.

As we have said, Leo wished to achieve a certain uniformity in the life of the church. But he recognized that there were limits to that uniformity. Although he desired uniformity in procedures, he felt some freedom to change liturgy so that it would be a part of the culture of the people worshiping.

Nevertheless, Leo did desire uniformity in certain aspects of worship. He wrote to the bishop of Alexandria concerning days for baptism and the number of times Communion could be celebrated on major feast days. We do not need to discuss the specific points Leo made, but he assumed that whatever Rome did represented the most ancient tradition; and he wrote with a firm sense of authority.

However, Leo really did not understand the theological significance Christians in Alexandria saw in their forms of worship; and the people there were not willing to conform to Western practice. Leo had tried to exercise more authority in the East than Eastern Christians felt he possessed. In this sense, Leo had made a clear step in the development of the medieval papacy and the claims that it made for authority over the whole church. This incident also demonstrated the resistance of the East to such claims. We will see more of this conflict in our next chapter.

The Significance of Leo's Leadership

Leo understood quite well that Christians constantly need nurture from the church in order to grow in their faith and to live out the implications of that faith. Only about a hundred and fifty years had elapsed since the church had been a persecuted minority in the Roman Empire. But Christianity had become the state religion, and the old religions of the Empire were outlawed about the time Leo was born (though some of these religions appealed to many people). The persecution had ended, but that did not mean that being a Christian was an easy matter.

The earlier religious persecutions seemed to bring out the best in the church. Without such opposition Christians were in danger of becoming lazy and complacent. Virtue rather than life was under attack in Leo's time; and the danger was greed, not the confiscation of goods.

Strife and dissension among Christians occur in times when the church faces no persecution. Instead of being tempted to sacrifice to idols, complacent Roman Christians were tempted to commit evil deeds. Persecution had its problems, but the lack of persecution was also a great danger for the church.

Leo sought to make the church a strong instrument of Christian education and support in order to prevent complacency. In this connection Leo realized that strong lines of authority and communication were necessary. Christians needed to know that they were part of the "one, holy, catholic church" and not some small, weak, local group of like-minded people. Leo's administrative task was to unify the church and to make it the same church all over the world, united by a common theology and by a common understanding of how the church ought to live its life. Leo saw his own office as the center of that unity. For this reason he felt he could exercise great authority over all other churches, especially those in the West.

Some Issues for Today

When we look at the church in our own time, we realize that Leo's concerns have a contemporary ring to them. We probably do not agree with the forms and structures Leo established or strengthened in order to attain his goals. But his objectives do relate to the church in the twentieth century in the United States.

Was Leo right in thinking that the end of persecution put the church in danger of great temptations? If

21

so, we need to be aware that our churches are in a situation of peace and acceptance far greater than that which Christians in the fifth century experienced. Have we become complacent as a church? Have we, even as those Romans, lapsed into cultural patterns that ignore Christian values?

Leo indicated that greed became a problem for Romans who no longer lived in fear that an antagonistic government would take their property. In our own culture money has indeed become a major influence on values. How should Christians respond to this situation?

We can look at the church in other countries around the world, many in places of persecution or difficulty. The church is growing in those places. In areas of the world where the church has been well accepted for centuries, the church is shrinking. Two hundred and fifty years before Leo, Tertullian (a great theologian) had said that the blood of the martyrs is the seed of the church. Leo understood that point. Complacency does not create a strong church.

As we have seen, Leo had several methods for strengthening the church. One method was to use the liturgy and the adminstrative life of the church for the purposes of Christian education and nurture. Leo felt that the danger of complacency and a decline in faithfulness could be overcome by sharpening the individual Christian's connection with the whole community of faith, strengthening the sense of identity, and reinforcing the values Christians are to hold. Leo emphasized this approach in his preaching. His references to the sacraments and the church year were for this purpose. In our own day, many Christians seem to feel that the church is unnecessary or that the church is more in need of their attendance than they are in need of the church's nurture. How can we reverse this trend?

In situations where the church is under stress, Christians feel the need to gather, to worship together, and to celebrate the sacraments. These activities are like daily bread for them, manna in the wilderness. But in situations of complacency, feeling this way about worship may be more difficult. Leo tried to overcome such attitudes. Do we face the same problems? If so, how can we go about changing these attitudes?

Leo also wished to strengthen the connections of all churches so that local congregations were not isolated. Do we also need that sense of connectedness, even beyond the bounds of a single denomination or a single nation? How do we accomplish that sense of connectedness in our day?

Leo's concern was for a church that was one, clearly united and therefore with sufficient uniformity to be able to be called "one." At the same time, as we can see from his changes in the liturgy, Leo understood the need for diversity. How do we deal with the need for adaptation of the church in our own culture and, at the same time, realize that we as Christians are part of other churches whose style of worship has also been adapted to fit their culture?

We all have the tendency to think our way of worship is the only proper one. Within the missionary movement in years past, "our" form of worship often became the normative form for new churches in cultures that were quite different from Western Europe and the United States. In recent years those "younger churches" have begun making their worship and practices clearly related to their culture. In what ways do our church structures and worship reflect our culture? To what degree does our church reflect cultures that are not ours? Do we need to do some of the same adaptation that the younger churches are doing?

---

[1]From *Leo the Great* and *Gregory the Great*, Vol. XII in A Select Library of Nicene and Post-Nicene Fathers of the Christian Church, second edition, edited by Philip Schaff and Henry Wace (Wm. B. Eerdmans Publishing Company, 1956); pages 196–97.

[2]From *The Book of Hymns*, No. 715.

3

Leo as Theologian

Leo's work as an administrator had enormous implications for the development of the church in the West and shows his excellent grasp of the principles of government and administration. However, his place in history is due far more to his work as a theologian.

Sometimes we think of the roles of a theologian and an administrator as quite separate. They were not for Leo or for any of the great leaders in the history of the church. In other words, the best administration in the church is carried out on the basis of solid theological understandings of the nature of the church and its gospel. And at the same time, the theological foundations of the church have the greatest impact when those foundations are involved in the shaping of the life of the community of faith through the actual decision-making structures of the church rather than remaining a matter of the intellectual life only.

Leo was an able theologian. He had the ability to see to the heart of a theological issue, to see what was essential to the gospel, and to see what endangered those essential concepts. He could articulate his points succinctly, clearly, and persuasively for clergy and laity alike.

The Theological Environment

In the mid-fifth century, several theological controversies were dividing the church. In some cases certain views had already been declared heretical.

Pelagianism was the name given to the teachings of the followers of Pelagius, a British monk who had found considerable following in Latin North Africa. The great theologian Augustine had spent the last years of his life opposing those teachings. Pelagianism asserted that all human beings are born sinless. They then individually decide to sin or not to sin but are usually overwhelmed by the examples of the sinful human beings all around them. The role of Jesus, therefore, was to provide a good example and to model the kind of life that each person could choose.

In opposition to this view, Augustine supported the doctrine of original sin, meaning that all people are sinful from birth and that the work of Jesus Christ is to free us from the bondage to sin, not merely to set an example. We require divine grace to be redeemed. Human decision alone is not enough, said Augustine.

Most of this controversy was in the Western part of the church, and various Western councils condemned Pelagianism. Leo constantly enforced the decisions of these councils and asked bishops to root out Pelagianism where it still existed. In fact, in a letter written after he became pope, Leo urged a bishop to check on reports of Pelagianism in his diocese.

Arianism was the form of Christianity some of the Germanic tribes practiced. Arians believed that the one who became incarnate in Jesus of Nazareth was not the one true God but was instead a lesser divine being, a creation of the Father. In 325, the Council of Nicaea declared Arianism a heresy. But through a variety of events, some Germanic tribes had been converted to Arian Christianity. These groups were not particularly concerned with the theological distinction between orthodox Christianity and Arianism. They wished to be Christian. Leo opposed Arianism, but he understood that he needed to win these groups to Roman Christianity by gentle persuasion.

The Background to the Christological Controversies

The Council of Nicaea had condemned the Arian position and stated that the one who became incarnate in Jesus of Nazareth was indeed the one true God, the only-begotten Son of the Father, of one substance with the Father, not a creature but God. Then new arguments arose.

Some persons were concerned about maintaining the full humanity of Jesus. Earlier in the history of the church a view had been put forward that Jesus was not really human but only appeared to be so. The term for this view was *Docetism*, from the Greek word for "to appear" or "to seem."

The doctrine of the virgin birth served as a safeguard against such a view. It stressed that Jesus had a mother and was born as a human child is born, without denying that Jesus' conception was also a miraculous act of God. Docetists held that Jesus was not born but appeared as an adult, seemingly but not really human. According to the Docetists, Jesus was God, wearing the clothes of humanity.

The church opposed such opinions, showing that these ideas led to a denial of the real death of Jesus on the cross. If Jesus were only God and not human, he could not have suffered and died; and the Resurrection would not have been a real resurrection if no real death had taken place. So, after the Council of Nicaea stressed the true and complete divinity of this Incarnate One, the issue arose as to how we can comprehend this Jesus as both fully human and fully God.

The earliest answer the church proposed was discussed and condemned at a council at Constantinople in 381. This view held that Jesus had a human body and soul but that his mind was divine. The divine Word was in the place of a human mind. But a human being without a human mind is not fully human. This solution was seen as a variation of Docetism. The council rejected this answer and stressed that the Redeemer is one of us as well as God. God's assumption of human nature in the Incarnation was a major part of the process of redemption.

This first controversy was largely in the Eastern part of the Empire, as was the second, settled in 431. This second controversy centered around the bishop of Constantinople, a man named Nestorius. He had claimed that Mary was the mother of the human nature of Jesus only, not of the Incarnate One who was both human and divine. The issue was not Mary but whether her child, the one to whom she actually gave birth, was human only or both human and divine. To Nestorius, the two natures were sufficiently separate that Mary could be called the mother of the human nature only. The divine Word, the second person of the Trinity, was closely associated with this human Jesus but by an agreement of wills, said Nestorius. The two natures were two persons, one human and one divine. Jesus was the human person with whom the divine Son agreed to be associated.

The Council at Ephesus in 431 regarded this opinion as a denial of the Incarnation. An association of two persons, one human and one divine, is not the same as God becoming human. Especially in the East and most strongly among monastics, great antipathy arose toward Nestorianism and to any notion that the human and divine natures in Jesus could be separated.

All this information is background for the time of Leo's papacy. The West had not been particularly involved in these struggles, though popes prior to Gregory had frequently acted as arbiters in debates centered in the East. These debates were the result of different theological emphases centered in Antioch and in Alexandria, the ancient patriarchal sees (the official jurisdiction or office of a bishop) of the Greek-speaking areas of the church. The rivalry had been complicated by the creation of a patriarchate (a major center of church administration) in Constantinople, the new capital of the Empire. Rome remained the only such patriarchate in the West.

Furthermore, the theology of the West did not have the same philosophical and speculative base as did much of the theology in the East. As we have seen, the West was more concerned with legal relationships, clear statements of doctrine, and structures. On the issues of Christology the West held to a formulation made by the great Latin North African theologian Tertullian a century and a half earlier.

Tertullian argued that "we see plainly the twofold state, which is not confounded, but conjoined in One Person—Jesus, God and Man."[1] The West believed that Jesus was one person of two natures, not two persons, as the Nestorians held. Neither did the West believe that Jesus had an incomplete human nature, a theory that had been refuted in 381 at the Council of Constantinople.

Leo was quite familiar with this traditional Western view that Jesus was one person of two natures, for an understanding of the Incarnation was foundational and absolutely central to his whole theology. Therefore, the conflicts in the East about Christology were important to Leo. He agreed with the decisions that had been made in 325 at Nicaea, in 381 at Constantinople, and in 431 at Ephesus. If a real incarnation—the true God actually taking on true humanity—had not taken place, then Leo believed that our salvation was in question.

Leo felt that for the Holy God to take on the form of humanity, even the form of a slave, was the greatest sign of God's love and concern for us. Leo wrote, "He took the form of a slave without stain of sin, increasing the human and not diminishing the divine: because that emptying of Himself whereby the Invisible made Himself visible . . . was the bending down of pity, not the failing of power."[2]

And again, in another sermon at Christmas, Leo said,

What mind can grasp this mystery, what tongue can express this gracious act? Sinfulness returns to guiltlessness and the old nature becomes new; strangers receive adoption and outsiders enter upon an inheritance. The ungodly begin to be righteous, the miserly benevolent, the incontinent chaste, the earthly heavenly. And whence comes this change, save by the right hand of the Most High? For the Son of God came to "destroy the works of the devil," and has so united Himself with us and us with Him that the descent of God to man's estate became the exaltation of man to God's.[3]

The Mid-fifth Century Controversies

The decisions made in the past were not final, however. More controversy broke out during Leo's pontificate. Again the center of the debate was in the East. In 448, a local council in Constantinople charged a monk named Eutyches with heresy. Eutyches was not an obscure monk. He was the head of a monastic community and was the godfather of one of the highest officials of the imperial government. However, though prominent in ecclesiastical circles, Eutyches was not theologically astute. He knew what he believed, and he was sincere in his beliefs. But he could be used by others for political ends, which is most likely what happened. Intrigue was high.

Eutyches's view was this: Before the Incarnation occurred, one could speak of a human and a divine nature that were to be joined in the Incarnation. But when the Incarnation occurred, the divine nature was so overwhelming that the human nature ceased to function. In a sense, the divine nature transformed the human nature into itself. Thus, the Incarnation came from two natures or out of two natures; but the Incarnate Jesus had one nature, and that one was divine. This opinion was later termed *Monophysite*, from the Greek terms meaning "one nature."

The local council condemned Eutyches and excom-

29

municated him. He appealed to Leo and to other patriarchs. Once the matter was clearly explained, Leo agreed with the condemnation. Leo wrote to Flavian, the patriarch of Constantinople who had presided at the council. In a fairly brief letter Leo said he agreed with the council and was sending a longer reply as soon as possible.

The promised longer reply was far more than a letter, and it has always functioned as more than a letter. This reply is generally referred to as Leo's "Tome." Leo wrote it to Flavian but then sent copies on later occasions to many other people. It is the clearest and fullest statement of his opinion on the major Christological issue of his time. And it has survived as one of the best such statements.

The Tome is a mere five pages long, and one page of that is not the theological statement but deals with specific matters about Eutyches. Yet, in the typical fashion of Leo the Tome condenses the balanced statement of the West's tradition. The heart of the matter is in these words:

> Without detriment therefore to the properties of either nature and substance which then came together in one person, majesty took on humility, strength weakness, eternity mortality: and for the paying off of the debt belonging to our condition inviolable nature was united with passible nature, so that, as suited the needs of our case, one and the same Mediator between God and men, the Man Christ Jesus, could both die with the one and not die with the other. Thus in the whole and perfect nature of true man was true God born, complete in what was His own, complete in what was ours. And by "ours" we mean what the Creator formed in us from the beginning and what He undertook to repair.[4]

This statement became central in later Western thought.

Leo knew that Eutyches was quite ignorant and

unlearned in theology, was aged, and had a previously unblemished life in monasticism. Leo urged Eutyches's readmission to the church as soon as Eutyches agreed with the opinion of the council.

A new and universal council was called to meet in Ephesus in 449. Leo could not go; but his Tome, already in the hands of Bishop Flavian, was the statement of Leo's belief and the condemnation of Eutyches. Leo sent two delegates in his place. About one hundred thirty bishops were present. They were surrounded by monks and soldiers who supported Eutyches. Leo's letter was not read; Eutyches was exonerated and restored. Flavian was declared deposed because of his former opposition to Eutyches. One of the delegates speaking for Rome, a young deacon named Hilary who would later be pope, refused to agree to the decision. He was the only one to do so. Great disorder and chaos ensued. The Roman delegates left.

What the Roman delegates did not know was that as the chaos continued, Bishop Flavian was badly trampled. In this condition he was put in prison and then exiled. Flavian died within a few days. When Leo heard the reports of the meeting, he immediately wrote to Flavian in support of his position and called the meeting no council of the church.

Not realizing Flavian was dead, Leo also wrote to the abbots of monasteries in the area around Constantinople, asking them to recognize no one but Flavian as their bishop. The patriarch of Alexandria gathered support from other bishops and declared Leo excommunicated. The emperor backed the position of the meeting at Ephesus and the new patriarch of Constantinople who replaced Flavian.

The Council of Chalcedon

Matters stood this way until all was unexpectedly changed in a moment. The emperor was riding his horse; the horse stumbled; and the emperor fell and was killed. His sister, the orthodox and very devout

Pulcheria, became empress. She was a friend of Leo.

A new council was called to meet in Chalcedon in 451. Again, Leo did not attend but sent delegates. This time Leo's delegates presided. About five hundred twenty bishops were present. The Tome was read, and a statement of faith that agreed with the Tome was drafted and signed. This statement is what is referred to as "The Definition of Chalcedon." Along with the creed from Nicaea, it forms the basis of the church's statement of faith about who Jesus Christ is and how Jesus Christ is related both to God and to humankind.

The members of the council debated Leo's position and agreed to it because they felt it was orthodox. Leo, as bishop of Rome, believed he had authority to define doctrine and no debate or vote on his doctrine was necessary. Clearly the difference of opinion on this matter was continuing and growing sharper. The council also decreed that the bishop of Constantinople was second in honor only to the bishop of Rome because Constantinople was the "New Rome." Leo never accepted this view, since to him Rome's pre-eminence was due to Peter's place at the beginning of the line of bishops in Rome. Constantinople had no such authority.

Further problems divided the church. Many Christians in Egypt, especially the monastics, did not agree with the decisions of Chalcedon. They separated from the rest of the church, partly because they disagreed with Chalcedon but also because they resented the increasingly Greek character of the Eastern church as dominated by Constantinople. The same pattern developed in other areas of the church, generally among groups such as the Syrians who were not Greek. To this day these churches survive and are called Monophysite churches.

Some Issues for Today

The decision at Chalcedon increased the stature of Leo as a theologian and as preserver of the tradition of the church. But Leo also watched Constantinople gain in prestige and some major ancient portions of the church become severed from the communion of the whole church over which Leo believed he presided.

Today we still face many of the misunderstandings that Leo worked so hard to undo. Many people in our churches have a very unclear idea of what they mean in saying that Jesus Christ is fully human and fully God but only one person. Yet, Leo was correct; the heart of our faith is based on *who* this Jesus Christ is.

What difference would it make to your faith to believe that Jesus was not fully human? What difference would it make to believe that Jesus was indeed only a human being to whom God the Son had agreed to be very closely associated? What do we celebrate at Christmas?

Look at the first chapter of the Gospel of John and think about how this study of Leo's theology can help us understand more fully the significance of the famous statement, "And the Word became flesh and dwelt among us" (John 1:14a). Leo's theological efforts are still important for us today.

---

[1] From *Latin Christianity: Its Founder, Tertullian*, Vol. III in The Ante-Nicene Fathers, edited by Alexander Roberts and James Donaldson (Wm. B. Eerdmans Publishing Company, 1957); page 624.

[2] From *Leo the Great and Gregory the Great*, Vol. XII in A Select Library of Nicene and Post-Nicene Fathers of the Christian Church, edited by Philip Schaff and Henry Wace (Wm. B. Eerdmans Publishing Company, 1956); page 40.

[3] From *Leo the Great and Gregory the Great*; page 140.

[4] From *Leo the Great and Gregory the Great*; page 40.

4

Gregory as Leader of the West

We know much more about the early life of Gregory than about that of Leo. Gregory was born into a wealthy and noble Roman family. He was expected to take his place in society and to play a significant role in civil affairs. To that end Gregory was educated, and his early adult years bore out the expectation of a life of public service for the common welfare. At one point Gregory served as a high public official for the city. His family was known for its Christian piety and devotion. Many of the women in the family lived under private forms of monastic discipline, and Gregory was related to two previous popes.

The family owned a considerable amount of land, both in Rome and in Sicily. As the oldest son, Gregory probably had experience in managing these estates. His later life shows a quite detailed knowledge of the issues and laws involved in landlord-tenant relationships.

Somewhere around 575, Gregory made a decision that may have been on his mind for years. He determined to give up his secular life and join a monastery. Gregory would have been in his thirties at that point. His father had recently died, and the inheritance and management of much of the family property had come into his hands. Gregory gave away or sold much of the property in order to create seven monasteries. Six of these monasteries were in Sicily, the seventh at the family home in Rome. Each monastery received enough land to support the monastic foundation. Gregory gave the rest of the money to the poor. Gregory himself went to live in the Roman monastery that he had begun, a monastery named Saint Andrew's.

Gregory wanted to be part of a community of monastics. He did not wish to be a hermit or to live a monastic life alone. The model of Benedict of Nursia was quite an influence on him. Evidently Gregory did not wish to be the head of the community in which he lived. Someone else was abbot. Gregory entered into such a life happily and was content. Gregory lived by some extremely austere and ascetic practices, especially regarding fasting, that may well have contributed to severe health problems that developed later in his life.

Gregory fully expected to remain in the monastery, away from worldly concerns and activities, throughout his lifetime. It was not to be, however.

Recalled to the World

In 579, a new pope was in urgent need of able and dedicated people to help him carry out his duties in the midst of a Lombard attack on Rome. The pope urged Gregory to leave the monastery, be ordained a deacon in the church in Rome, and then go as a special papal ambassador to the imperial capital in Constantinople. Gregory's basic task was to gain help from the Empire for the increasingly difficult situation in Rome.

Gregory did not wish to enter into this activity; but the pressure was great, and the demand was clear. So, he agreed. Gregory was ordained and left for the capital, but he requested that a few other monks accompany him so that he could continue as far as possible in the monastic life that he had entered with such enthusiasm. Gregory remained in Constantinople until around 586. During that period he also spent time in writing and meeting many church officials from both East and West. This experience would be useful in Gregory's later role in the church.

However, Gregory was not able to gain much help for Rome. The emperor did not have troops to spare. Eventually, the pope realized that Gregory could be more useful at home. The pope gave Gregory more responsibilities in Rome, but permitted him to live at Saint Andrew's.

In 590, the pope died. Plague had taken his life as well as the lives of many others. Plague was only one problem; floods had already caused great misery. Famine was expected because granaries had been destroyed. In such a situation and with the need for a strong administrator, an experienced diplomat, and a dedicated and devout bishop at the head of the suffering church, the choice of the city for pope was Gregory.

Gregory did not wish to be elected pope. He wrote to the emperor asking him not to approve this appointment. But Gregory's own brother, a high civil official in Rome, destroyed the letter and sent to the emperor only the fact that the city unanimously elected Gregory. The emperor approved. Thus, against his own wishes Gregory was the new pope. He had sincerely hoped to be a monk and not to be involved in the administration of the church at large. His desires did not count; the times were against him.

Gregory's first task as pope was to deal with the natural calamities that were besieging the city. In that respect his duties were officially greater than Leo's had been. After a reconquest of many portions of the Western half of the empire by the Emperor Justinian beginning in 533, the imperial government recognized that it could not manage the civil affairs of the West without some assistance from the church. Distances were too great between the capital and the outlying Western areas. The civil government was still fragile because of the repeated invasions. Corruption was

everywhere, for the capital could not provide sufficient oversight. In contrast, the Western church was
well organized, had bishops in every major city, could
be on the lookout for injustice and for corruption, and
had a direct channel to the imperial structure in order
to keep things going well.

Therefore, in 554, Justinian issued a "Pragmatic
Sanction" to give bishops a voice in the selection of
civil governors and to guarantee weights and meas-
ures in trade. In addition, Rome had historically
maintained a public grain supply, to be doled out by
the city. The city's supply of grain came largely from
state farms in Sicily. The church had additional grain
supplies from church lands. But the city's granaries
had been destroyed in the disastrous floods. As a
result, much of the grain supply came from church
sources; and Gregory was in charge of those. He was
therefore intimately involved in the civil government
of the city.

Gregory also recognized that the new duties of
bishops required that bishops be effective administra-
tors, that they be able to deal with issues outside the
church as well as within it. Increasingly, Gregory
became involved in selecting local bishops and in
removing bishops who were incapable of performing
in this wider role or who did not deal with injustice
and corruption in the areas under their jurisdiction.
This process strengthened the centralized character of
the church, streamlined its machinery, made lines of
accountability clear, and put Gregory in the position of
recommending a great number of bishops throughout
Italy and Sicily. Furthermore, to make sure that the
process was working well, Gregory put in his own
direct inspectors, called rectors. These persons served
as his eyes, ears, hands, and voice in major areas of the
church.

Even more significantly, Gregory often chose these
people from the monastic community rather than
from the clergy who were not members of monastic
orders. This approach led to increased centralization,
since Gregory made these appointments directly,

by-passing local clergy with local interests and power bases. This way of doing things also blurred the lines between monastic life and the life of clergy. Gregory had considerable success with this process of central- ization in Italy and in Sicily; but his policy left a certain resentment in the local, nonmonastic clergy who often felt that they had been demoted in favor of the representatives from Rome.

Gregory could not act in the same way in North Africa, Spain, or Gaul. Local traditions were strong; and the authority of the bishop of Rome, while great in many respects, was not as capable of direct involve- ment in the day-to-day workings of the local church.

Gregory's Role in Civil Society

Gregory had enormous problems to face as the result of the Lombard invasions, the floods, and the breakdown of the ability of the imperial government to be of much help in dealing with these situations. The church had to provide grain for the populace, and the structure for distributing grain was also through the church. Refugees were a great issue as well; these people had serious needs for financial and other support that had to come from the church. At one time three thousand refugee nuns who had fled from the Lombards were in Rome.

At least forty episcopal sees were vacated during the Lombard invasions. That is, the bishops were not present and the cities had ceased to function as the residences of bishops. Gregory had to decide where the administration of the area would be centered and what bishop would be in charge of the churches. Sometimes priests were active, but they had no bishop. Who would be their bishop? Discipline could break down seriously in such a situation.

Furthermore, some priests and bishops had migrat- ed to safer places and had brought with them silver and gold sacred vessels and other valuables. Many of these clergy were selling these vessels in order to live. Gregory wanted to put a stop to this practice. He wanted to have such wealth recorded by the church in which these people were now located in order that the vessels could be returned to their original churches when the Lombards withdrew. Gregory made one exception, however. He ruled that church wealth could be sold by the proper bishop in order to ransom people the Lombards had taken captive.

What was the role of the relocated bishops? Who was in charge of the priests who came with them: the bishop who came with them or the bishop of the place in which they now resided? All these questions were difficult administrative issues that Gregory had to face.

Rome was filled with hungry people, refugees and Romans alike. Gregory made sure that the church prepared food and took it into the streets to the sick and the poor who had no other source.

Gregory was an inveterate letter writer; 854 of his letters remain. Most of these letters deal with investigating charges of corruption, with specific instances of injustice, and with disputes between landlords and tenants, especially tenants on the church lands. Gregory was concerned about charges of short weights being used with peasants. He was aware of grain shipments and the problems in ports that slowed grain deliveries from Sicily. Gregory sent his officials to check on all sorts of reports of seizures of land, overstepping of bounds by officials, and so forth. He was intimately involved in the daily life of churches throughout Italy.

Gregory aimed his efforts at protecting the peasants, insuring honesty in trade, and maintaining clear property titles. He returned money that the bishop of Syracuse in Sicily had sent to be used for the poor in Rome, commenting on the number of people in Syracuse who needed help. Gregory was wary of gifts that might imply currying favor with the pope.

The imperial troops stationed in Rome had not been paid and were restless. Gregory paid them from the church treasury. When Rome was under siege by the Lombards, Gregory negotiated a treaty when supplies of grain in the city were exhausted. Famine was the only alternative. Many Romans had been taken into slavery in Gaul. Gregory paid five hundred pounds of gold to end the siege. Gregory honored the emperor as the head of the government. However, for all practical purposes Gregory was the government, not only in Rome, but for a large part of Italy.

Issues Within the Church

Gregory was pope during a time of several theological conflicts within the church. The Lombards were Arians. The wife of the Lombard king was a Roman Christian, however. Her son became king in 591. The Lombards accepted him even though he was a baptized Roman Catholic. Gregory sought to work through the queen for the conversion of the whole Lombard people. But at the same time many Lombard nobles were planning to attack the Romans. Gregory did not let the political problems overshadow his ultimate goal of having the Lombards as part of the Roman church. His goal was reached within a century after his death.

A schism took place in the north of Italy among those people who felt that imperial decisions to which the popes had agreed had compromised the issues clarified at Chalcedon during the time of Leo. Here too Gregory worked to bring about a healing. This goal also was achieved completely after his death. Gregory did not alienate the groups involved in various controversies. He tried to bridge the gaps, to work toward a future harmony, and to lessen the enmity.

Gregory continued writing, and his works were essential for the theological education of priests in the centuries after him. His later letters often mention the great pain he endured. Among other things, he suffered from gout and spent much time unable to leave his bed.

Gregory wrote the *Pastoral Rule* that set forth ways of dealing with the spiritual problems of the wide variety of people a pastor is likely to see in a church, especially in confessions. This document shows psychological sensitivity and pastoral concern, not simply a legalistic handling of sins. The book also shows that Gregory assumed a highly structured society, hierarchically organized, with specific duties and responsibilities at every level. In this respect Gregory was typically Roman.

Gregory has often been cited as the source for the development of the form of Western church music called "Gregorian chant." Pope Gregory II in the eighth century may deserve more of the credit. However, Gregory the Great may have had a role in paving the way for this later development. Gregory's process of centralizing the church and the increased influence of monastic forms naturally led to increased uniformity in liturgy. However, even though Gregory was a strong supporter of monasticism, he was quite sure that church deacons, who were part of the staff of city churches, should not spend their time in chanting the liturgical services several times a day. They had much work to do in helping the poor and needy. Therefore, Gregory set up a *schola cantorum*—a special group for singing—so that the deacons could go on with their regular work. In this sense, Gregory may have set the stage for the later development of liturgical music through the establishment of a group specializing in singing.

The authority of the bishop of Rome in the church throughout the world was of concern to Gregory. He continued Leo's struggle against any assumption that the patriarch of Constantinople was close to an equal with the Western patriarch. The lines of division were growing clearer between the Eastern and Western churches.

The Significance of Gregory's Role

Gregory had not sought the office of pope. He was not personally interested in power and prestige. In fact, he had given up everything to move away from a life that had such characteristics in order to take up a

41

life of poverty and monastic obedience. Even as pope, he maintained as much as possible the style of life of a monk. To this end he surrounded himself with other monastics whom he trusted.

Once in the office of pope and faced with the needs of the church and the society around him, Gregory used the office to its fullest. He was a reformer wherever discipline had broken down or wherever people were overlooking the common good in favor of private gain. Gregory's method of reform was centralizing the church, appointing to offices those persons who were well qualified. These persons were often fellow monastics.

Some Issues for Today

In our own day we may have difficulty imagining centralization as a major means of reform. We live in an age when people resent centralized bureaucracy in the church as well as in society. Reform seems to imply decentralization.

We need to recognize, however, the character of the times in which Gregory lived. The central government of the Empire had virtually collapsed in the West. Even in the church, chaos was everywhere. In Gregory's mind, and probably even in ours had we been there, centralization seemed the clearest way to provide the unity and organization needed to deal with the problems of the time. Yet, Gregory also began the process that led to the medieval papacy and with it the dangers that strong centralized structures can bring. The Protestant Reformation was a response to abuses of power to which such centralization contributed.

However, a more interesting issue is the degree to which the church can find itself in a situation in which the church needs to deal with some of the problems of the wider society. Was Gregory right in negotiating and concluding peace treaties with the Lombards? Should bishops have had the task of reporting corrupt civil officials to the emperor? What about giving out grain to the Romans and ransoming captives taken by the Lombards? What about refugees and the hungry? Gregory used the structures of the church to deal with all these issues.

What would this kind of activity look like in our own day? Our civil government is democratic rather than imperial. Does that fact change the role of the church? Do emergency situations demand that the church respond when the civil government cannot or will not do so? What kinds of events or situations in our own day could call forth responses parallel to the response of Gregory? The issue is the relation of church and state and the role of the church in the wider society. We are to some degree inheritors of the tradition in which Gregory stood even though our governments and our churches are structured differently than his.

Hunger, refugees, and peace—these were constant concerns of Gregory the Great as a faithful Christian and as a leader of the church. They are issues that Christians today face as well. Our situation and our responses may be quite different than his, but we cannot avoid the problems any more than he could. In studying Gregory's responses, we may find some help in framing our own.

5

Gregory as Missionary and Theologian

Gregory's Roman world was shrinking. The Lombards were quite strong in Italy. The Goths were dominant in what had been Roman territory. Britain was no longer a functioning part of the Empire. Some Romans may have felt that the end of the world was near since the end of Rome seemed at hand. And so Gregory thought.

As head of the Western church, what was one to do in preparation for the return of Christ? We have already seen one answer: Be sure the church is uncorrupt, functioning well, and disciplined in life and in administration. But a second response was to preach the gospel as far and wide as possible, especially among the peoples who had recently come into contact with Rome precisely because of the invasions that were destroying the Empire.

Gregory had seen this need for missions even before he became pope. But he did not have the power then to carry out this mission, since he was in a different role with different responsibilities. However, once he became pope, he could begin to carry out this task with vigor. And so he did.

Gregory tried to convert the Lombards from Arian to Roman Christianity through the Lombard queen and her son, who were Roman Christians. Gregory also wrote to the Visigothic king in Spain, applauding his action when he changed from Arian to Roman Christianity. Gregory tried to end the ancient forms of pre-Christian worship carried on by some peasants who worshiped at shrines on hilltops. Gregory insisted that baptized Christians not revert to previous lifestyles and that non-Christians be encouraged to be baptized.

Clearly, Christianity was a fairly light veneer on the surface of an ancient agricultural society that still maintained in many ways its earlier religious forms. This situation was especially the case in Sicily and in the other Italian islands. Gregory's authority was quite strong in the church-owned lands that were extensive in Sicily. But in other areas Gregory could only urge and recommend.

Gregory tried to do so persuasively. He also tried to persuade the Frankish queen—the Franks were Roman Christians—to eliminate the pre-Christian practices in her realm.

Gregory's attitude toward Jews was that the civil law allowed their religious practices, and the law must be upheld. However, Gregory encouraged Jews to convert to Christianity and recommended inducements for them to do so.

These issues were administrative matters in areas that were already largely Christian. Gregory's major work as a missionary went beyond these concerns, however.

The Mission to Britain

A story told in an early eighth-century account of Gregory's life and popularized after that relates that Gregory became interested in missions to Britain when he saw some Angle slaves in Rome. The story involves a series of plays on words, for instance, that the Angles looked like angels. However legendary that account may be, Gregory probably did learn from Anglo-Saxon slaves about the situation of Christianity in Britain. From his correspondence with Christians in Britain, a more intentional plan of mission emerged.

A Christian queen in Britain, Bertha, was married to the king of Kent. She was Frankish, and the marriage agreement permitted her not only to continue to practice her faith but also allowed her to bring a bishop with her. She had a chapel, and services were conducted there.

Gregory was also aware that ancient forms of Christianity still existed in parts of Ireland and Wales. Other than the Kentish queen, Gregory had no reason to assume the church was functioning in the areas of Anglo-Saxon conquest that had overrun the older British and Roman society. He found little evidence of mission from the conquered to the victors or mission from the queen's chapel to the people.

We need to pause and look at the process that these Anglo-Saxon tribes were undergoing, for their social forms were also developing. These people had been members of tribal groups that lived by conquest, moving from one place to another. But in Gregory's time their lives were changing. They were beginning to settle down in the areas of Europe they had conquered and were developing the forms of society that went with more settled life. The Franks had undergone this process earlier, at which time the king had become a Christian, bringing the nation with him. The same thing had happened in Spain with the Visigothic king. Now the Kentish king had married a Christian queen. But no one seemed to be pressing the issue of the extension of the church in that area. Perhaps the time was ripe for a mission from Rome to urge the king to permit such activity within his realm.

For this purpose, Gregory organized and sent forty monks. This approach again emphasized his reliance on monastics for much of his work. The group was headed by a man named Augustine, known in history as Augustine of Canterbury in distinction from the great North African theologian of the fourth and fifth centuries, Augustine of Hippo. Augustine was well-known to Gregory as the prior of Saint Andrew's, and the monks who went to Britain were also from Gregory's former monastic home.

Augustine and his group left Rome for Britain in 596. They got as far as Gaul; but there they stayed, frightened by the stories they heard of the wild land to which they had been sent. Augustine left the others and went back to Rome, but Gregory would not agree to abandoning the mission. Gregory sent Augustine back after naming him abbot of the monastic group. So, Augustine had additional authority over the monks. Gregory also gave Augustine letters of commendation to various bishops in Gaul through whose territories the group would go and whose assistance the monks might need in the future.

We do not need to give the details of the story of Augustine's mission. He was successful. He did preach before the king, and a way was made for the mission to proceed in Britain. The king himself was soon converted and baptized. Many of his subjects followed him in that decision, but no force was used. In fact, the king prohibited the use of force and permitted the ancient religions to continue. The decision to become a Christian was not compulsory in Britain as it had been in other tribes when the king had decided to take that step.

Augustine's mission grew to the point that Gregory arranged for him to be consecrated as an archbishop, and Augustine went to Gaul for that purpose. This appointment gave Augustine authority over all other bishops in Britain. Of course, Augustine did not know how many other bishops were active in Britain. He had little contact with the older British Christians or with the increasing Irish mission that was spreading from the northwest. The Irish mission was not dependent on Rome in any way. Eventually these missions would meet, and their differing forms and structures would cause conflict. But that is a later story.

Gregory was deeply involved with that British

mission. His character and methods are clear in his correspondence with Augustine. As we have already seen in the hesitancy of Augustine and his party to continue their mission, Augustine needed the support and encouragement of Gregory as he began his work.

The situation was not easy in Britain. How should Christian leaders deal with customs and practices that were part of that society but not allowable under Roman Christianity? What was essentially Christian and what was merely Roman culture in the forms of the church that the missionaries were bringing with them? Augustine needed guidance on such matters. And so he wrote to Gregory.

In one letter Augustine described miracles that had occurred through his ministry. These miracles helped convert the people. Gregory wrote back, pointing out that miracles were promised to Christ's followers. Then Gregory reminded Augustine that God used weak people to proclaim the gospel and that Augustine ought not to take any pride in what had happened: "And whatsoever thou mayest receive, or hast received, in the way of doing signs, regard these powers as not granted to thyself, but to those for whose salvation they have been conferred upon thee."[1]

The most famous part of this correspondence is a letter in which Gregory replied to specific questions that Augustine asked about his work in Britain. Though the letter bears the marks of some later editing, the letter is essentially Gregory's. This letter circulated among later missionaries and has had an important place in the history of missions.

Augustine asked eleven questions. The first dealt with how the bishop should budget the wealth that the church receives from the faithful. Gregory's reply indicated that he was passing on the tradition of Roman bishops. Gregory's response has been quoted widely. John Calvin used it with favor against the spending policies of the Roman Catholic Church of the Reformation period.

Gregory divided the proceeds into four parts. One

fourth was for the bishop's household, which included the entertainment and hospitality that went with that role. One fourth was for the support of the clergy under that bishop. One fourth was for the poor, and the final fourth was for the repair and upkeep of church buildings. Gregory also urged Augustine to continue the practice of the bishop living in community with the clergy as far as possible.

In response to another question, Gregory added that lower clergy who wished to marry should receive stipends separately so that they could establish their own households.

Augustine was confused by the forms of worship that he had discovered in Gaul and that did not agree with the custom of Rome. Gregory's reply was quite instructive and applied directly to Augustine's situation in Britain:

> Thy Fraternity knows the use of the Roman Church, in which thou hast been nurtured. But I approve of thy selecting carefully anything thou hast found that may be more pleasing to Almighty God, whether in the Roman Church or that of Gaul, or in any Church whatever, and introducing in the Church of the Angli, which is as yet new in the faith, by a special institution, what thou hast been able to collect from many Churches. For we ought not to love things for places, but places for things. Wherefore choose from each several Churches such things as are pious, religious, and right, and, collecting them as it were into a bundle, plant them in the minds of the Angli for their use.[2]

Gregory's advice shows an astonishing freedom that he was willing to give to Augustine. Gregory understood that Roman practices were not to be considered universally applicable and that certain adaptations would be necessary. He also understood that other churches, such as the church in Gaul, may well have developed some forms of worship that were excellent and that should be commended to the Anglo-Saxons as they began to develop their own forms of worship. Simply because a form was from Rome did not make it either the only or even the best form for others to use.

The church had long governed marriages between Christians. Augustine was concerned about the levels of family relationships that could prohibit marriage, that is, what constituted incestuous marriage? The customs in Britain were different than those in the Empire. Furthermore, what ought to be done about the people who were already married to persons the church would prohibit Christians from marrying but who were seeking baptism?

Gregory made a distinction between Roman law and biblical injunctions given to Israel and worked out a fairly brief list of those people who could not marry. Those persons who were already so married ought to understand that their unions were not in accord with the will of God, but they should not be prevented from receiving baptism and Communion. Gregory wrote, "For at this time holy Church corrects some things with fervour, tolerates some things with gentleness, connives at and bears some things with consideration, so as often to repress what she opposes by bearing and conniving."[3]

At a later date Gregory wrote a letter to an abbot who was being sent with several monks as additional help to Augustine. This letter changed some of the advice Gregory had given earlier. He had said that shrines of idols were to be destroyed when the people had turned to Christ. Now Gregory suggested keeping the old temples, removing the idols, and consecrating the buildings to the worship of the true God. In addition, he said that Christian feasts ought to be scheduled on the dates when the people were accustomed to having festivals and celebrations. Gregory wrote, "For it is undoubtedly impossible to cut away everything at once from hard hearts, since one who strives to ascend to the highest place must needs rise by steps or paces, and not by leaps."[4]

50

In dealing with all these issues, Gregory showed a strong pastoral sensitivity and an ability to understand the significance of cultural issues as well as essential theological concerns. His wisdom was so significant that a later missionary monk, Boniface of the eighth century, would request a copy of this letter to help him with his endeavors in Germany. Boniface was a product of the monasteries that the Roman mission had developed in Britain. Gregory's letter to Augustine became an essential document for medieval missions.

Gregory as a Theologian

Gregory was not a particularly original thinker. He made a deliberate attempt to avoid the more academic, classical forms of Latin in order to write in a fairly colloquial fashion so that all people could understand him. Gregory's concerns were always pastoral. He stressed miracles and holy people who showed the power and validity of their faith.

Part of this approach may simply have been Gregory's own interest. But some of this interest may have been caused by the new audience that was always in his mind: the Germanic peoples who were new to the Roman faith.

Gregory's writings include accounts of miraculous events that people could regard as proof of the value of faith and the virtuous life. Gregory collected these stories from a variety of sources and was not particularly interested in the historical facts behind them. He provided material for much of the medieval "lives of the saints" literature that was a major vehicle of popular Christian education.

Gregory faced few significant theological debates. Even the Arian tribes represented more of a social and political division than a theological one, and their ready switch to the Roman side illustrates that fact. But this state of affairs does not mean that no significant theological issues arose from Gregory's writings.

Gregory picked up on a theme that had been in the Christian tradition for some time, that is, that the sacrament of Communion is a sacrifice. The Mass is an unbloody repetition of Calvary. Gregory did not invent this idea, but he used it extensively and clarified what had been a somewhat ambiguous statement of the character of this sacrifice. Drawing on Gregory's writings, the medieval church increasingly built its sacramental theology around this central idea. This approach represented a major shift in the church's view. Emphasis moved more and more to the sorrow and sacrifice of Good Friday and less to the joy of Easter Sunday. The fast every Friday took on great significance.

According to Gregory, judgment is imminent, sin will be punished, and therefore the forgiveness brought by the sacraments is essential. Gregory had a legalistic view of the payment required for sin, and the sacrifice of the Mass was the major way to deal with this necessary payment. Life is fragile; death can come at any moment. Security is not possible in this life, so devotion that reminds us of death and prepares us for it is central for the Christian.

Gregory transmitted these concepts to the generations after him. He became the major theologian for the training of priests in the Middle Ages. Even the earlier theologians were read by later centuries through the lens of Gregory's theology. In that way, Gregory became a pivotal theological figure.

Some Issues for Today

The temper of the times has an obvious influence on theology. In Gregory's day the situation of instability, invasions, flood, famine, and plague led to the stress on death and judgment that we mentioned above. What is the temper of our time and our culture? How does that temper influence the kinds of theology or the interpretations of the Christian faith that we see around us today? How strongly should such factors influence theology? How can we prevent them from being too dominant? What happens when the cultural mood changes and the theology does not?

Gregory's work as a missionary remains one of his major contributions. He was able to think in terms of a mission toward precisely the groups that were ending the Roman Empire that was his home. His response to the chaos of the time was not despair or inactivity. He did not think only of his own safety. Rather, he turned his efforts to the work of spreading the gospel. What are the situations that we can imagine for ourselves that might parallel Gregory's missions to Germanic groups?

In his letter to Augustine in Britain, Gregory set forth several principles for adapting the church to that culture and showed that he did not feel bound to impose Roman forms everywhere. Look at the principles that Gregory set down, as we have seen them in this chapter, and consider how we could apply them in our own churches today. Was Gregory too lax in enforcing standards on those who wished to come into the church? Are we as concerned about missions as he was? Why, or why not? How do we go about spreading the gospel?

Gregory's concern about non-Romans had a strong effect on his whole outlook and theology. Does a sense of mission keep our focus on those persons who are outside our culture and church?

---

[1]From *Gregory the Great, Ephraim Syrus, Aphrahat*, Vol. XIII in A Select Library of Nicene and Post-Nicene Fathers of the Christian Church, second edition, edited by Philip Schaff and Henry Wace (Wm. B. Eerdmans Publishing Company, 1956); page 75.

[2]From *Gregory the Great, Ephraim Syrus, Aphrahat*; page 75.

[3]From *Gregory the Great, Ephraim Syrus, Aphrahat*; page 76.

[4]From *Gregory the Great, Ephraim Syrus, Aphrahat*; page 85.

6

The Legacy From Rome

Leo and Gregory were two of the most significant leaders of the Western church between the fifth and the eleventh centuries. Part of their importance lies in the fact that few great theologians and leaders emerged in those difficult and turbulent times. But these two people would have been outstanding in any generation. The times called forth qualities of leadership that a more settled period might have allowed to remain unused.

The decisions these popes helped to make remain important for us as well. Leo's theological work regarding the nature and person of Christ is a touchstone of Christian doctrine for the church even today. Both popes were important for the development of the papacy, and we have noted their efforts in that direction.

Losses and Gains

The decision of the Council of Chalcedon in 451, strongly dependent on the writings of Leo, led to a schism in the church. This division was permanent. Increasingly, Constantinople was the center of a Greek church that had lost important non-Greek areas to the separate structure of the Monophysite churches (see Chapter 3 in this book), especially in Egypt and Syria. People in these areas were unhappy with the strengthening of Greek ties and the loss of their own regional leadership. Greek bishops had been appointed to non-Greek areas, and this practice caused resentment. The church was only paralleling what had already happened in the civil government in the East. All these events were bad signs for the health of the church as well as for the Roman Empire.

While the influence of the Orthodox Church in the East was diminishing, the time of Gregory brought about a rather different situation in the West. The church was spreading in the West. Not only were Arians turning toward the Roman church, through Gregory's missionary efforts new groups such as the Anglo-Saxons were being added. Through these people other Germanic groups would enter the church in future years.

Though Gregory had a tendency to expect other people to conform to Roman practices, he was sensitive to cultural differences and permitted these differences to be lived out in the church. Therefore, the West was in many respects becoming more diverse both as a church and as a culture precisely at the time when the East was becoming increasingly uniform.

In the midst of these opposing tendencies and shortly after the death of Gregory, one of the great events of history occurred, an event that changed everything for the church and for the Roman Empire. That "event" was not a single occurrence but the whole rapid series of conquests that marked the beginning of Islam and the development of the Moslem world. The significance of the decisions made earlier at the time of Leo and Gregory would only now be fully appreciated.

Gregory died in 604. Mohammed died in 632. Between Mohammed's death and 732 when Islamic forces were defeated at Tours in southern France by the Frankish leader Charles Martel, the entire region from just south of Constantinople through the ancient Christian areas of Syria and Egypt came under Moslem domination. This region included the ancient patriarchates of Antioch and Alexandria. Islam provided a vehicle for Arab conquest and nationalism, and it was a powerful movement indeed.

From the ancient areas of the East, Islam had rapidly spread westward. North Africa fell, and Moslems captured its ancient Christian center of Carthage. Few persons in the region remained Christian. The dominant non-Roman population became Moslem. The islands in the Mediterranean were under Moslem sway, cutting off the traditional communication by sea. Much of Spain was conquered, and Gaul was threatened until the Battle of Tours.

Much of the region that was the ancient stronghold of Christianity was no longer the home of a flourishing church. Constantinople remained intact and would remain so for many centuries to come. But the city was even more than ever the capital of a Greek state and church and was located at the far eastern tip of its jurisdiction.

In the West, Rome remained a strong center. Its future lay where Gregory had labored in mission. But Rome was a church center; it was no longer the state center. Rome was at the southern tip of its sphere of influence. However, the city remained strong due to alliances it had forged with the barbarian invaders. To these peoples the church brought the ancient Roman civilization, now combined with the Germanic heritage to bring forth a new European church and society, a church and society strong enough to survive and thrive despite the Moslem threat.

Seen in this light, the importance of Gregory's work cannot be overestimated. He had no idea of what was coming. In fact, what Gregory anticipated was the end of the world and the Second Coming. His work in strengthening the church was the result of his faithfulness in that situation. Yet, Gregory's work provided an unexpected future and hope for a church that might otherwise have been almost totally destroyed.

Mission probably always works best in such a situation. Some kinds of mission are self-serving, such as a local church seeking more members in order to meet its financial obligations. Such a church reflects no real joy in new members who are different and who bring their own cultures and gifts. Real mission is difficult in such circumstances.

Gregory urged mission for the sake of those he sought to bring to Christ. And he permitted them to remain non-Roman and to be different. Gregory did not know how useful these people might be in the future of the church. But he did realize how useful the church might be to these people.

Leo and Gregory's Roman Limitations

Even the most able and forward-looking leaders cannot be free of the culture in which they live, and they cannot be completely aware of the impact of that culture on them. Both Leo and Gregory viewed society as naturally hierarchical, a characteristic of Roman culture. At some points their Christian faith was able to break through, but they retained many Roman sociocultural assumptions that remained unchallenged in their work.

The best example of this problem is found in the work of Leo. We have seen the stress Leo put on the great act of God—the Mighty, High God—who became one of us in the Incarnation. The love and humility of God are astonishing, and Leo centered his theology on this willing humiliation of God who not only became human but became a lowly human. God the Son took on the form of a slave, a servant.

Yet even with this theological stance, Leo was a creature of his time. In one of his earliest letters as pope, he wrote to bishops in various provinces in Italy to outline rules for ordination and complained, "Men are admitted commonly to the Sacred Order who are not qualified by any dignity of birth or character: even some who have failed to obtain their liberty from their masters are raised to the rank of the priesthood, as if sorry slaves were fit for that honour; and it is believed that a man can be approved of God who has not yet been able to approve himself to his master."[1]

Slavery was a fact of life. Slavery had long been practiced in the Empire. And with the barbarian invasions, slavery was even more common, since the invaders considered slaves and hostages as major rewards of conquest. The church had long urged that masters give their slaves freedom or at least allow slaves to purchase their freedom. Such acts were considered righteous and helpful for the state of the master's soul. Clearly the church saw some conflict between the gospel and slavery though it did not condemn slavery outright. Leo here spoke of slaves who had not appeared to merit receiving their freedom.

But Leo saw no contradiction between the great act of God in becoming a slave and the church, preaching that gospel, refusing ordination to someone who was born a slave. Jesus would not have qualified for ordination because his birth was too lowly! Leo's view of God and his view of society came from two different sources and never seem to have met. Leo believed priests were members of society and should be from the appropriate ranks of that society in order to maintain the high status of the clergy and the church.

However, God is not concerned about such matters. Indeed, had God been as concerned about appearances as Leo, the Incarnation may have occurred in the person of a prince or high priest or some ranking member of the community. But it did not. God came to us in the form of a servant, a lowly person, not even from the capital city, but from the hinterlands of Palestine and from the family of a carpenter.

What we have here is a clash between the content of the gospel and the social expectations of a particular culture. Leo was an excellent interpreter of the gospel but was so bound to his culture at some points that the astonishing message of the gospel was lost in the society of his time. What would have happened if the church of Leo's day had embodied in its life as the church the surprising character of God's action toward us? Doing so might have permitted the church to challenge the whole institution of slavery far earlier than it did.

Leo was not alone, however, in such inconsistencies. Our own churches have similar ideas about what is appropriate. We often have unspoken qualifications both for ministry and membership that have more to do with social standing in secular terms than we would like to admit. We are probably as unable to imagine the full significance of the Incarnation we celebrate for our church and our world as was Leo. We too have cultural assumptions that we keep insulated from the gospel.

Gregory's theology also shows the marks of being Roman. He stressed precisely the most Roman forms from the earlier theology of the West and lost some of the characteristics less typical of Rome. Nowhere can we see this approach more clearly than in his stress on the death of Jesus. Of course the cross has been central to Christian theology from the beginning. But in Gregory the legal character of Western thought is obvious. According to Gregory, God is the Legislator and Judge of the universe. Humankind has broken the law and has been judged. The penalty is death. The death of Jesus Christ is the payment for sin, given by a perfect human being in our place, so that the payment has been made and we are allowed to live. That this One who died as a payment for sin is also God shows the great love and pity of God. The Incarnation is for the purpose of payment. The sacrament of Holy Communion is in some way a repetition of this sacrifice that continues to pay for the sins of the world.

The entire structure of this theology is legal and judicial. It has the flavor of a court of law from start to finish. In earlier theology this approach was an occasional theme, but in Gregory it became the central and dominant one. Earlier interpretations almost

59

disappeared. This approach has continued to be the major stress of the Western churches. Though Protestants would differ with Roman Catholics on the repetition of Calvary in the sacrament, many would still agree with the basic form of the theology: The death of Jesus Christ is a payment for sin against God. That concept is the heart of the substitutionary understanding of the Atonement.

But other interpretations, both in Scripture and in early theology, point in different directions. The cross is the final conflict between God in human form and all the forces of evil that sin allowed to have dominion over this world. The cross appears to be a defeat for Christ, but the Resurrection shows the great victory. We, by faith, may now live out of that victory rather than living as though evil still were triumphant.

Both understandings are in Scripture. But clearly the first one is more in line with the Roman penchant for legal forms and interpretations. In the West in general and in Gregory in particular, this form became the only one. As a result, the variety and richness of earlier theology were generally lost. Only recently have we in the West regained that earleir richness.

Later Followers

The names *Gregory* and *Leo* became popular names for popes after these two people first used them. We cannot assume that the names by which popes choose to be known can tell us a great deal about who they are or what they intend to accomplish in their holding of this office. But two later popes—both among the greatest in the history of the papacy—each chose one of these names; and their lives and actions seem to indicate that they felt themselves called to follow the example of one of these earlier popes.

Gregory VII was the other great pope by that name. He became pope in 1073 and died in 1085. Gregory VII followed very much the method of Gregory the Great in using the centralized authority of the papacy for the purpose of the reform of the church. Under Gregory

VII the church experienced the "Gregorian Reform." This reform sought to end the buying and selling of church positions. It also sought to eliminate the power of secular officials over the appointments of bishops and other church leaders.

Gregory VII was a strong pope in his use of power. Like his earlier namesake, he saw the significance of the monastic life and continued and expanded the influence of monasticism on all the clergy. Even priests not in monastic orders were increasingly expected to imitate the monastic life as far as possible. The model of the earlier Gregory was quite strong indeed.

Leo XIII was one of the greatest of the modern popes. His pontificate lasted from 1878 to 1903. Leo XIII came to the papacy at a time when the Western world was becoming increasingly secular. Scientific discoveries and democratic institutions increased the sense that humankind had great power and could look after its own interests better than could a monarchical church that seemed old-fashioned to many people.

New problems were on the horizon, such as disputes between labor and management in the new industrial cities and poverty on a new scale caused also by industrialization and the ending of rural societies. The Roman Catholic Church had been out of touch with this new society since the French Revolution in 1789 because the antichurch character of that revolution had frightened the Roman Catholic Church into a fortress mentality rather than one of engagement with the world.

In the midst of the church's movement toward rejection of the world and its problems, Leo XIII became pope. He was as conservative as his predecessors in regard to the authority of the pope. But like Leo I, he was sure that what the church needed above all was a theology that was accurate, persuasive, and able to engage the world in which the church actually lived. Roman Catholic theology at the end of the nineteenth century was more concerned with repetition of accurate statements than with creative theological engagements with the problems of the time. Leo insisted that all students for the priesthood be exposed to the best theological minds, especially that of Thomas Aquinas, the great thirteenth-century theologian who had opened up the church of his day to the currents of thought that challenged traditional thinking.

Leo's hope clearly was that such a solid theological base could give the church the necessary means by which it could address the problems of the modern world. In fact, a fairly straight line runs between the theological renewal Leo XIII began and the renaissance in the Roman Catholic Church that has occurred in our generation, even though Leo could not foresee the directions his beginning would take in later years.

Models of Reform

In looking at the two great leaders in Rome in the fifth and sixth centuries as well as glancing at their later namesakes, we can see that Gregory and Leo illustrate two modes of church reform. One is administrative, largely through centralization. The other is theological, the rediscovery of the heart of the faith and the difference it can make for all of life. But we cannot say that Leo was only interested in theology and that Gregory was only interested in administration. We have seen that these popes were involved in both theology and administration.

As we said at the beginning of this study, we may disagree with the form of government that these popes assumed. We may even differ to some degree with the theology they professed. But we have the same task of combining our theology and our ways of living as the church, just as they sought to do.

We have also seen that Leo and Gregory were not always consistent. Sometimes they let their culture define the gospel rather than allowing the gospel to evaluate and challenge their cultural presuppositions. We face that problem as well. Seeing their limitations may help us raise questions about our own.

In spite of their limitations, however, we have seen that both popes felt the church must be a part of the culture of the people it serves even if the church does need to question that culture. Leo and Gregory sought to give freedom for adaptation of the church among the different ethnic and cultural groups that became part of it. We also face this challenge. Our world is far more varied than the ancient world; and the church has spread far beyond the confines of the Roman Empire, as Gregory hoped that it would.

The issue of diversity and unity is our problem as well as theirs. How can we believe that we are all part of "the one, holy, catholic church," the body of Christ, when we are all so different? When we look at how these two Christians, so far from us in time, struggled to deal with these issues, we may gain the courage to deal with them ourselves.

---

[1]From *Leo the Great and Gregory the Great*, Vol. XII in A Select Library of Nicene and Post-Nicene Fathers of the Christian Church, second edition, edited by Philip Schaff and Henry Wace (Wm. B. Eerdmans Publishing Company, 1956); page 3.